£2·40

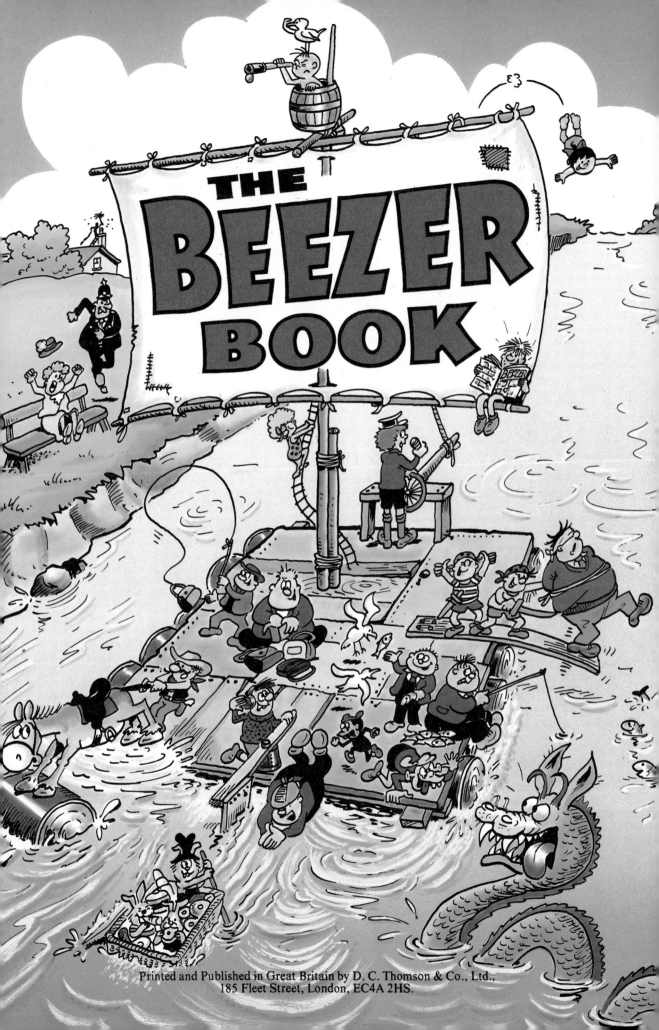

THE BEEZER BOOK

Printed and Published in Great Britain by D. C. Thomson & Co., Ltd.,
185 Fleet Street, London, EC4A 2HS.

A shower of fun with the red-haired one!

GINGER

I LOVE SWIMMING.

BUT A NICE SHOWER AFTERWARDS IS EVEN BETTER.

Suddenly—

OOF!

OUT OF MY WAY. I SAW THIS SHOWER FIRST.

ROTTER! BUT NEVER MIND. THERE'S ANOTHER ONE.

But—

AAIEE! I'VE SLIPPED!

SLIP!

And—

BAH! SOMEONE ELSE HAS TAKEN THE SHOWER.

Things don't go well at this hotel.

THE BADD LADS

I'LL PUT THIS ON THE LAWN.

NOW I'LL GO BACK INSIDE AND WAIT FOR A THIEF TO COME ALONG!

Soon after—

THERE HE IS! GO GET HIM, TINRIBS!

But then—

OUCH!

HO-HO! THAT TIN TWIT'S BITING POP INSTEAD OF CHASING THE THIEF!

OH, NO! HELP!

CALL IT OFF, SOMEBODY!

HEY! WHERE'S THE GRANDFATHER CLOCK?

THERE IT GOES, MUM!

HA-HA! IT'S A DOG'S LIFE, POP!

CHOMP!

CRUNCH!

Dan makes a mistake when he tries to bake.

BEEFY DAN
THE FAST-FOOD MAN

DAN, YOU'RE GETTING LAZY! HOW ABOUT MAKING SOME COOKIES?

YAH! MISSED AGAIN!

So—

I'VE MADE COOKIES LIKE THE BOSS SAID.

PHEW! THEY'RE MIGHTY HEAVY!

Shortly—

AH! DAN'S MADE COOKIES AND LEFT THEM OUT TO COOL. I'LL TRY ONE.

But—

WOW! WHAT A WEIGHT!

THOSE COOKIES WERE LIKE LEAD! MAKE THEM LIGHTER!

HUNGRY HOSS

I'M STARVING. I'LL LOOK ROUND TOWN FOR SOME GRUB.

STORE

SALOON

Then—

IT'S FEEDING TIME, LITTLE BIRDS.

I'LL HAVE SOME OF THIS BREAD.

But—

BEAT IT, YOU VARMINT. THAT BREAD'S FOR BIRDS, NOT FLEA-BITTEN HORSES!

HM! I'VE GOT AN IDEA. THIS CALLS FOR A POW-WOW WITH MY INDIAN FRIEND.

So—

HOW, FLEET FOOT! CAN YOU DO ME A FAVOUR?

ANYTHING YOU WANT, HOSS.

And soon—

HEE-HEE! I'LL PASS AS A BIRD WITH THESE FEATHERS AND FLIPPERS!

Later, in town—

I'VE GOT A NICE BOWL OF FOOD FOR THE BIRDS.

Outside—

CHIRP! CHIRP!

WOW!

HELLO! IS THAT THE ZOO? THERE'S AN UNUSUAL SPECIMEN OF BIRD OUTSIDE. IT'S PROBABLY DOWN FROM THE MOUNTAINS. IT EATS LIKE A HORSE!

Meanwhile—

THIS IS LOVELY GRUB!

But then—

HEY! WHAT'S GOING ON?

CHIRP! NEIGH! CHIRP!

STORE

ZOO

HM! THAT SOUNDS LIKE HOSS IN THAT ZOO TRUCK!

ZOO

I'D BETTER GO AND SEE WHAT HOSS HAS BEEN UP TO.

And—

HA-HA! IT MAKES A CHANGE FOR ME TO BE GETTING YOU OUT FROM BEHIND BARS, BIRD-BRAIN.

DO NOT FEED

BAH! THIS REALLY GIVES ME THE BIRD.

Just take a look at this ' scrap '-book!

SCRAPPER

LOOK! HERE'S THE DIARY I'VE KEPT SINCE THE FIRST OF JANUARY.

I HAD TO CLEAR AWAY SNOW—NOT EXACTLY SPIFFING FUN!

HO-HO! BUT I HAD LOTS OF 'BIFFING' FUN.

EEK!

OW!

HELP!

THERE WERE A LOT OF FALLS IN FEBRUARY.

HOI!

HEY!

YES! AND I CAUSED MOST OF THEM!

MY HAT!

I THOUGHT THE WIND WOULD NEVER STOP BLOWING IN MARCH.

OOF!

I GOT IN A FEW GOOD 'BLOWS' MYSELF.

IT RAINED ALL THROUGH APRIL.

YEAH! AND I 'RAINED' PUNCHES ON BASHER BILL.

BAH! ALL I DID WAS DIG, DIG, DIG IN MAY.

OW!

I GAVE LANKY LANE A GOOD 'DIG' IN THE RIBS.

IT WAS TOO HOT IN JUNE.

WELL, I COOLED A FEW PEOPLE DOWN.

I DID ENJOY GOING FOR A PADDLE IN THE RIVER IN JULY.

I DID A BIT OF 'PADDLING', TOO.

AUGUST WAS A DISASTROUS TIME FOR ME WITH MY CRICKET BAT.

HO-HO! I THINK I WAS A BIG HIT WITH MINE.

EVERYTHING WAS DAMP AND MISERABLE IN SEPTEMBER.

ESPECIALLY TUBBY TATE AFTER I KNOCKED HIM INTO A PUDDLE!

I WASN'T ANY GOOD DUCKING FOR APPLES AT THE HALLOWE'EN PARTY IN OCTOBER.

WHEE! BEEFY BROWN WASN'T MUCH GOOD AT 'DUCKING' EITHER.

PUZZLE

1—This colourfully-dressed gentleman is properly known as a Yeoman of the Guard and can be seen guarding the Crown Jewels in London. Do you know his more familiar nickname? Is it: (a) Beefeater? (b) Grenadier Guard? (c) Royal Archer?

2—Flies beware! This plant actually feeds on small insects. It attracts them with its sweet smell and traps them on its sticky leaves. Is it a: (a) Bee Orchid? (b) Spotted Flycatcher? (c) Sundew?

3—Isn't this a strange creature? Abou eighteen feet long, it lives in the Arcti Ocean, and its huge tusk is thought to b used for defence. It feeds on squid, fis prawns and shrimps. Is it a: (a) Porpoise (b) Killer Whale? (c) Narwhal?

4—You won't see many people riding these today! It was one of the early forms of bicycle. Is it called a: (a) Boneshaker? (b) Penny Farthing? (c) Tandem?

5—If you lift up a flat stone, you might find fearsome-looking beetle. But don't be alarmed. harmless—and doesn't have a sting in its tail! Is i (a) Devil's Coach Horse? (b) Colorado Beetle? Deathwatch Beetle?

PICS

6—Do you know the name of this neck of land on the west coast of Scotland? A famous pop singer wrote a song about it. Is it called the: (a) Kyle of Lochalsh? (b) Mull of Kintyre? (c) Firth of Forth?

7—This wild flower can grow up to five feet high, and is found all over the country. After the Second World War, it grew profusely on bomb-sites. Is it: (a) Fireweed? (b) Cowslip? (c) Purple Orchis?

8—The Beauchamp family was responsible for the building of this famous English castle in the fourteenth century. Is it called: (a) Windsor Castle? (b) Glamis Castle? (c) Warwick Castle?

9—This bird is not a good flier, but it is an exceptionally fast runner. It lives on the plains of south-western U.S.A. where it is known to attack and eat rattle-snakes! Is it a: (a) Roadrunner? (b) Crested Coua? (c) Pheasant?

ANSWERS

6. (b) 7. (a) 8. (c) 9. (a)
1. (a) 2. (c) 3. (c) 4. (b) 5. (a)

THE BANANA BUNCH

GRRR! FATTY'S WEIGHT BROKE OUR BED. WE'LL NEED A NEW ONE NOW.

AS FROM NOW, YOU'RE ON A DIET, FATTY!

Later—

PLEASE DON'T PUT ME ON A DIET, BRAINY. I'LL STARVE!

WE'VE LOCKED OUR FOOD IN THE PANTRY—OUT OF YOUR WAY.

I'LL JUST BURST THE PANTRY DOOR OPEN AND HELP MYSELF TO SOME GRUB.

HO-HO! I THOUGHT HE'D TRY THAT!

AAAARGH!

I'VE MADE THE PANTRY BURGLAR-PROOF!

WAAH!

HO-HO! BRAINY FITTED A SPRING TO THAT PANEL!

CHEERIO, FATTY! HEE-HEE!

OUCH!

Fatty shoots out of the tunnel and lands on the bedspring.

WAAH!

AAAA—

—AARGH!

Inside the hut—

OH, NO! HE'S LANDED IN THE PANTRY!

PANTRY

MUNCH! MUNCH!

GET HIM OUT BEFORE HE SCOFFS OUR GRUB!

GULP! I CAN'T. THE DOOR'S LOCKED AND I'VE LOST THE KEY!

YOU CLOT! WE CAN'T EVEN BURST THE DOOR OPEN!

HO-HO! I CAN EAT AS MUCH AS I WANT. THE BUNCH CAN'T GET IN TO STOP ME!

Meanwhile—

GRRR! COME BACK HERE!

STEADY ON, LADS! I LOSING THE KEY WAS AN ACCIDENT!

The NUMSKULLS

I'VE BEEN INVITED TO A REUNION OF MY OLD SCHOOL PALS. I CAN HARDLY REMEMBER THEM.

I CAN HARDLY REMEMBER THEM!

MEMORY SCREEN.

BRAIN DEPT.

I'LL JUST GIVE HIS MEMORY A JOG BY SHOWING A FEW PICTURES.

So—

FATTY FENWICK

SKINNY SIMPSON

SMILEY SMYTHE

CURLY DONALD

YES! IT'S ALL COMING BACK TO ME. I WONDER IF THEY'VE CHANGED AT ALL.

Then—

OH, NO! MY SUIT'S LIKE A DOG'S DINNER.

IT'LL BE ALL RIGHT IF HE GIVES IT A SPONGE AND A PRESS.

BRAIN DEPT.

MY SUIT'S LIKE A DOG'S DINNER!

GIVE IT A SPONGE AND A PRESS

SUGGESTION BOX

Then—

IT'S TAKEN QUITE A TIME TO DO THIS. I'LL HAVE TO HURRY.

But—

BAH! IT'S RAINING! I'LL TAKE MY BROLLY.

Soon—
THE RAIN'S GETTING HEAVIER. I'LL BE SOAKED BY THE TIME I GET TO THE REUNION.

Then—
I'LL TELL HIM TO TAKE A SHORTCUT.
BRAIN DEPT.
TAKE SHORT-CUT THROUGH BUILDING SITE!
SUGGESTION BOX

So—
I'LL TAKE A SHORTCUT THROUGH HERE.
BUILDING SITE

But then—
AARGH!

Some time later—
I USED TO BE A REAL FATTY UNTIL I WENT ON A DIET.
PEOPLE CAN'T CALL ME SKINNY ANY MORE. I TOOK UP BODY BUILDING.
AND I LOST ALL MY CURLY HAIR.
I'M SMILEY. BUT I LOST ALL MY TEETH.

Then—
WE'VE ALL CHANGED A LOT —BUT THERE'S SOMETHING THAT'S STAYED THE SAME.

HA-HA! LOOK AT THE MESS HE'S IN. HE WAS ALWAYS THE SCRUFFIEST BOY AT SCHOOL.
YEAH! HE DIDN'T GET CALLED 'SCRUFFY' FOR NOTHING.

AH, WELL! HE GAVE EVERYONE A GOOD LAUGH. HEE-HEE!
HA-HA!
HA-HA!
AND WE HAD A GOOD TIME, TOO.

Fruit hoot!

A tale about cheese that's sure to please!

BEEFY DAN
THE FAST-FOOD MAN

THOSE HAMBURGERS SMELL GOOD, DAN.

I'M GLAD YOU LIKE 'EM, BOSS.

I'LL LEAVE THIS LOT HERE WHILE I FRY SOME MORE.

COO! GRUB! I'LL TELL THE OTHERS.

And—

YUM! I CAN'T WAIT TO GET STUCK INTO THIS LOT.

Soon—

I'M LOOKIN' FORWARD TO THIS BURGER.

Suddenly—

MUNCH! THIS IS DELICIOUS!

Then—

I HEAR SOMEONE SNORING.

IT'S COMING FROM YOUR HAMBURGER.

THAT'S FUNNY. IT'S STOPPED.

I'LL JUST HAVE TO CLEAR THE TABLE WITHOUT TOUCHING THE DISHES WITH MY HANDS!

I'LL LIFT THEM WITH MY MOUTH INSTEAD.

Then—

SMIFFY, GET YOUR MOUTH OFF THAT PLATE.

OO-ER, OKAY, MUM!

I KNOW! I'LL CARRY THE TABLE INTO THE KITCHEN ON MY BACK!

HO-HO! THIS IS A GREAT IDEA!

But—

OH, NO! THE TABLE'S TOO WIDE TO FIT THROUGH THE DOORWAY. NEVER MIND! I HAVE ANOTHER IDEA!

OUR SHERIFF'S AN APE!

COYOTE CREEK is normally a nice, quiet town in the Wild West for it has two sheriffs to keep the peace. One is a normal bloke called Danny Blain—but the other is Danny's pet, a huge ape called Charlie.

BE A BIT MORE CHOOSEY ABOUT YOUR STAFF, MISTER CREEDY. THAT'S THE SECOND TIME THIS WEEK THAT CHARLIE'S FOUND WANTED CRIMINALS WORKING FOR YOU!

BUT THOSE TWO ARE MY COOKS.

CROOKS, YOU MEAN! THEY'RE WANTED FOR ROBBERY.

JUST BE A BIT MORE CAREFUL OR I'LL CLOSE YOUR PLACE DOWN.

GRR! HIM AND THAT OVERGROWN MONKEY ARE GETTING TOO BIG FOR THEIR BOOTS.

Catching crooks is very hungry work and Charlie had only one thought on his mind as he patrolled the town later that day— food!

Suddenly, the huge ape's eyes opened wide. Someone had been dropping bananas.

YUM-YUM!

Charlie's long strides ate up the ground—and he ate up the bananas!

At last he came to the end of the trail.

In more ways than one! A blow on the head knocked him cold.

—And when Charlie recovered he was frussed up like a turkey.

JUST YOU STAY THERE, YOU BIG APE.

HUH?

Some time later, Blinky Bradley was stumbling up a dark alley.

Suddenly—

IS THAT YOU, CHARLIE? WHAT HAVE YOU BEEN DOING IN THE BANK?

That's when Blinky found out the meaning of 'hard cash'! The hairy thief swung his bag of loot and Blinky went out like a light!

OW!

Meanwhile, Danny was getting a bit anxious about his pal.

I WONDER WHERE CHARLIE IS. IT'S NOT LIKE HIM TO BE LATE.

I'LL HAVE TO GO AND LOOK FOR HIM.

Then—

WOW! WHAT'S THIS? HEY! IT'S OLD BLINKY BRADLEY!

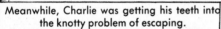

Meanwhile, Charlie was getting his teeth into the knotty problem of escaping.

Soon—

HUH!

Now no one makes a monkey out of Charlie and gets away with it. He raced out of his prison shack, determined to find his attacker. Instead, he found the posse!

THERE'S THE BANK ROBBER NOW. ARREST HIM.

CHARLIE!

So

JUST HOLD IT RIGHT THERE, CHARLIE. I'LL HAVE TO PUT YOU IN JAIL UNTIL I GET TO THE BOTTOM OF THIS.

HUH?

Soon the hairy sheriff was locked up in a tiny cell.

NOW, DON'T CAUSE ANY TROUBLE. I'VE GOT A LOT OF INVESTIGATING TO DO.

Charlie was miserable. No one seemed to believe he was innocent.

As he stared out through the bars, Charlie suddenly caught sight of a man going into the hotel. And there was something very familiar about his shirt! The head-banger had worn a shirt just like it.

GRR!

CREEDY'S HOTEL

The huge ape was determined to catch the man and no cell was going to hold him back, so—

UMPH!

Then—

HEY! HOW DID HE GET OUT OF JAIL?

The angry sheriff stormed into the hotel. But then—

IT'S THAT APE! FILL HIM FULL OF LEAD!

Charlie was as hard as iron, but he didn't fancy stopping any lead. He took to his heels.

With bullets whizzing round his ears, he leapt into the saddle of a horse hitched to a rail.

HUP!

Charlie gave a tug on the reins— and the whole rail came loose!

HE'S LET MY HORSE FREE. WHOA, TRIGGER!

In the confusion that followed, the jail-breaker made good his escape.

EEK!

OW!

HELP!

WHAT HIT ME?

WHOA!

Charlie headed for the hills. He was in big trouble and he needed time to think.

He also needed food. He searched in the saddlebags of the horse he had 'borrowed'.

That's when he found the bananas! He was just going to gobble them up when a thought struck him. They were the same kind as the ones that he had been following!

Charlie put two and two together and came up with a very painful answer.

BADLAND'S BANANAS

The horse clearly belonged to the crook with the club, so Charlie slapped it with a banana skin and off it ran. The ape hoped it would lead him to the crook's hideout.

The horse headed straight back towards town. Charlie raced after it. He
had to see where it finally stopped.

And that's when he got a shock. The nag pulled up
outside Creedy's hotel!

The hairy sheriff couldn't risk going in the
front door again so he decided to find a
back way into the hotel.

Then—

HO-HO! WE GOT THOUSANDS
OF DOLLARS FROM THE BANK AND
EVERYONE THINKS THAT CHARLIE
DID IT, MISTER CREEDY.

THAT'S RIGHT, MICK—THANKS
TO YOU CLOBBERING CHARLIE
AND ME WEARING THIS
APE SKIN!

HA-HA!

Charlie had seen enough. He
shinned up a nearby tree.

He swung his powerful body up . . .

. . . and then down! Straight through the window.

AAGH!

AAIIEEE!

Danny Blair was searching for clues when he heard roars and squeals of pain.

SOMEBODY'S IN TROUBLE! LET'S GO.

GRR!
HELP!
OW!
GRR!
EEK!

Then Charlie came into view, dragging the two crooks behind him.

CHARLIE! YOU'VE GOT THE CASH FROM THE BANK! THOSE TWO MUST BE THE REAL ROBBERS.

When Danny found the ape skin he knew what had happened. Charlie was completely innocent! The bank manager was delighted to get his money back and—

HERE'S A LITTLE REWARD. YOU'LL BE ABLE TO BUY YOURSELF SOME BANANAS.

But Danny had other plans for the reward money.

SORRY, CHARLIE BUT YOU DAMAGED THE JAIL. THIS'LL HELP TO PAY FOR IT.

BAH!

Lots of mishaps with burglar traps!

Suddenly—

YEOW!

BAH! FANCY HAVING A HUGE HOLE LIKE THAT IN THE GARDEN. I'LL GRAB THIS ROPE AND PULL MYSELF OUT.

Then—

ZONK!

OOYAH!

BAH! NOW I'M COVERED IN MUD. MAYBE I CAN BORROW A CLOTHES BRUSH FROM MISSUS SMITH.

But when he presses the doorbell—

URGH!

GRR! SOMEBODY'S PLAYING TRICKS HERE. I'M COVERED IN INK NOW.

Then—

I'LL CLIMB IN THROUGH THIS WINDOW.

But—

ERK! THE COAL BUNKER'S ON CASTORS!

Here's a silly billy! He thinks chili's chilly!

COLONEL BLINK

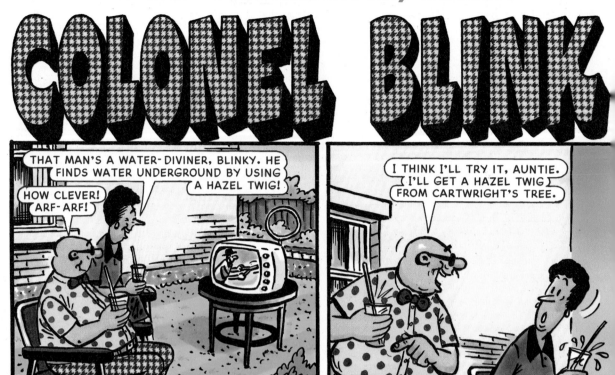

GRRR! YOU DID THAT TO ME ON PURPOSE! WELL, YOU CAN HAVE IT BACK!

PARDON?

I SAY, MADAM. KEEP YOUR HAIR ON. I DIDN'T DO ANYTHING!

IDIOT!

That hook's catching Blinky's shoe.

DID YOU SEE THAT, SIR? THAT WOMAN HIT ME WITH HER WIG!

Suddenly—

I'LL BE SAFER OUT AT SEA, AWAY FROM THAT TWIT WHO HIT ME WITH THE SEAWEED.

WAAH! GERROFF! SOMETHING'S PULLING MY LEG!

HEY! YOU'RE STANDING ON A BIT OF MY BOAT.

HELP!

HOP!

Soon after—

HELP!

THAT SOUNDS LIKE BLINKY'S VOICE! I'D BETTER SEE WHAT'S WRONG!

BLINKY! YOU SAID YOU WERE GOING WATER DIVING, NOT WATER SKI-ING!

STOP! WAAH!

HO-HO! THE MAN IN THE BOAT DOESN'T KNOW THAT HE HAS BLINKY IN TOW.

BEEZER

REDHWARA 1
TRIFUNERU 2
INOTSETARY 3
ARFOWTOE 4
TRELELACI 5
OYTS 6

1—Ginger wants to take the lift to the toy department upstairs but he doesn't know which floor it's on because the names are jumbled up. Can you help him unscramble them?

2—Mo and Mirabelle are admiring the table lamps. There is a design on each shade which changes in a certain pattern from left to right. See if you can work out what design should be on the fourth lamp.

3— Six little Numskulls are hidden on these pages. See if you can find them.

4—The Beezer artist has made 10 deliberate mistakes in drawing this Santa's Grotto. Can you spot them?

SANTA'S GROTTO

COMPUTAR GAMES

SNAKES LADDERS

DRAUGHTS

TEEZERS

5—Dick and Harry are helping Pop look for the Menswear department. Turn 'Mens' into 'Wear' in four moves, changing one letter each time to form a new word.

MENS

WEAR

6—Blinky thinks these dummies all look the same, but only two are, in fact, identical. Which two?

1   2   3   4   5

7—The Bunch only have enough money for one pair of socks. Brainy thinks the one who has the fewest number of pairs should get the new socks. He has one pair less than Tiny who has two pairs more than Fatty. Dopey has one pair more than Lanky and two pairs less than Tiny. If Brainy has 5 pairs who should get the socks?

Laughs for you with Saucy Sue!

I'LL TAKE OFF MY BIG OVERCOAT.

AND MY SMALL OVERCOAT.

AND MY JACKET.

AND I THINK I'LL TAKE OFF ONE OF MY CARDIGANS.

THAT'S BETTER. AYE, IT'S A GRAND VIEW FROM UP HERE, EH, SUE?

IT CERTAINLY IS, NOW THAT I'VE GOT A DECENT HIGH SEAT!

Smiffy has a lucky break — and no mistake!

SMIFFY, GO AND COLLECT MY VASE FROM AUNTIE MAY, AND DON'T BREAK IT.

OKAY, MUM!

And so—

BE CAREFUL GOING HOME WITH YOUR MUM'S VASE, SMIFFY!

DON'T WORRY, AUNTIE MAY.

But then—

OH, NO!

UNLESS I JUMP OUT OF THE WAY, THOSE CYCLISTS WILL RUN ME OVER.

ROAD UP

PHEW! I MOVED JUST IN TIME!

ROAD UP

AND MUM'S VASE IS STILL IN ONE PIECE!

ROAD UP

Soon after—

HEY! WHAT'S THAT, SMIFFY?

ER ... IT'S A VASE, BASHER!

A tick-tock shock!

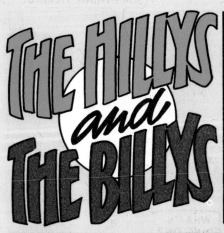

THE HILLYS and THE BILLYS

The sheriff of Happy Valley sleeps soundly.

ZZZ!

Suddenly—

BANG! BANG! BANG! BANG!

WHASSAT?

BAH! IT'S THE HILLYS AND THE BILLYS FEUDIN' AGAIN! IT'S THE SAME EVERY MORNING!

BANG! BANG!

Soon—

HEY! QUIT THIS FEUDIN'!

CLEAR OFF!

YEAH! WE'RE ENJOYING OURSELVES!

SHERIFF'S OFFICE

GRR! I'LL STOP THEM YET, DEPUTY.

Then—

HM! I'VE JUST HAD A GREAT IDEA!

So—

I'LL PUT MY CLOCK IN THIS CRATE!

Next day at dawn—

WE'VE NO AMMUNITION LEFT SO WE'LL INVITE THEM BILLYS TO JOIN OUR CLUBS. HEE-HEE!

But—

HEY! THERE'S SOMETHING TICKING!

TICK! TICK!

MAYBE IT'S A BOMB!

WOW!

LET'S GET OUTA HERE!

WHAT'S GOING ON?

TICK! TICK!

WOW! IT'S TICKING!

A BOMB!

TICK! TICK!

Later—

HO-HO! NOT A HILLY OR A BILLY IN SIGHT.

HA-HA! THEY DON'T KNOW IT'S JUST A CLOCK! I'VE STOPPED THEM FEUDIN'!

A CLOCK? WE'VE BEEN TRICKED.

Then—

PAW! IT'S A TRICK! THE SHERIFF PUT A CLOCK IN THE BOX!

WHAT?

LET'S PLAY A TRICK, TOO.

HO-HO! THIS REAL DYNAMITE WILL CATCH THE HILLYS NAPPING!

You're sure to grin when the Bunch sleep in!

Minutes later—

After school—

Later—

YOUR PLAN WORKED, BRAINY. WE'RE ALL AWAKE BRIGHT AND EARLY.

COCK-A-DOODLE-DO

RIGHT! LET'S GET UP AND DO OUR LINES!

I'VE FINISHED! IT'S TIME FOR SCHOOL NOW!

LET'S GO!

And so—

MORNING, SIR! HERE ARE THE LINES YOU ASKED FOR!

WELL DONE, BOYS!

Later—

HO-HO! THE BUNCH WERE UP SO EARLY THAT THEY'VE FALLEN ASLEEP.

WAKEN UP, BOYS!

YAWN! IS IT TIME FOR SCHOOL ALREADY?

NO! IT'S TIME TO GO HOME!

GRR! TEACHER GAVE US MORE LINES TO DO BECAUSE WE FELL ASLEEP IN CLASS!

IT'S BRAINY'S FAULT! THAT COCKEREL WOKE US UP TOO EARLY!

The MUNCHERS

Down below—

COUGH! START DIGGING! I'VE AN IDEA.

Much digging later—

NOW LET'S HEAD FOR THE SURFACE.

And—

PERFECT! RIGHT UNDER FARMER'S WIFE'S WASHING.

Meanwhile—

HAR! THEM MUNCHERS SHOULD APPEAR ANY SECOND NOW.

But—

TAKE THAT, YOU FOOL!

BAM!

LOOK WHAT YOU'VE DONE! YOU'LL HAVE TO DO THE WASHING AGAIN!

NEE-HEE! FARMER'S PLANS TO CATCH US HAVE GONE UP IN SMOKE!

The NUMSKULLS

And—

LET'S LIE IN THE SUN, TOO, LADS.

GOOD IDEA, BRAINY.

Soon—

EVEN IF THAT RABBIT LANDS ON OUR MAN AGAIN, WE WON'T GET TOSSED ABOUT.

But suddenly—

AAGH!

GROOH!

SORRY, OLD MAN. I WAS JUST WATERING MY GARDEN.

YOU IDIOT! YOU SOAKED ME.

FOLLOW ME! I'M GOING TO TELL OUR MAN TO BUILD A FENCE.

WHY DON'T YOU TELL HIM TO GO INTO THE HOUSE?

Then—

A BIG FENCE WILL KEEP EVERYONE OUT.

BRAIN DEPT.

IT SEEMS A LOT OF HARD WORK. I STILL THINK HE'D BE BETTER SITTING IN THE HOUSE.

BUILD A FENCE. HAMMER FENCE POSTS IN FIRST

SUGGESTION BOX

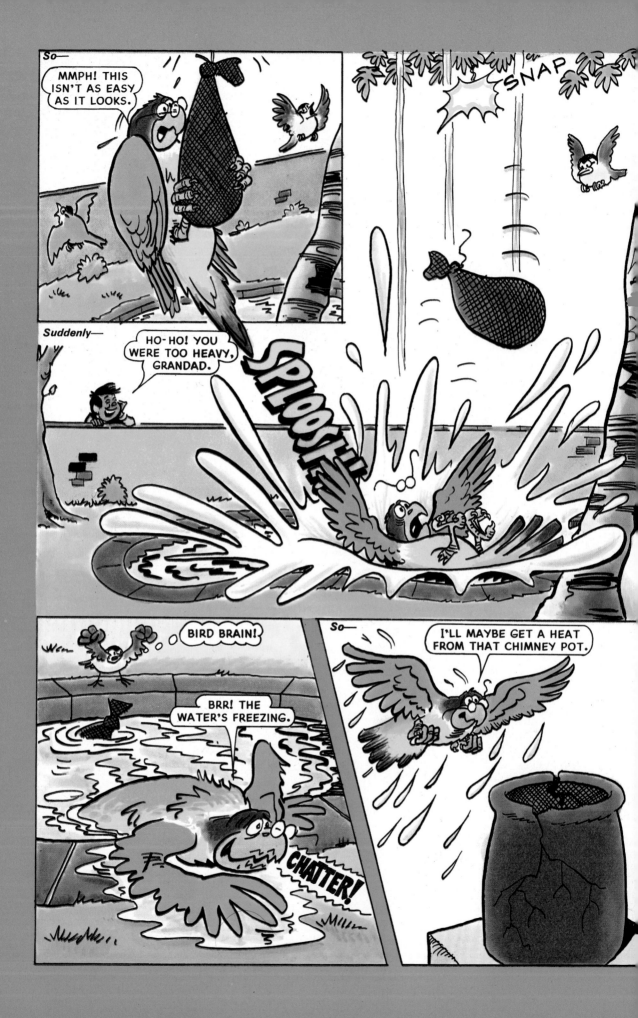

The Hillys are a mess but far from ' armless '!

Next morning—and everyone's asleep!

Well, almost everyone!

WE'RE GONNA FIX THOSE BLUNDERBUSSES!

SSH! QUIETLY DOES IT!

CEMENT

Later—

YAH! THE BILLYS ARE SOFTIES!

WHAT'S GOIN' ON?

THE BILLYS ARE BONEHEADS!

BOO TO

GRR! GRAB THE BLUNDERBUSSES, MEN!

THEY DON'T SMELL TOO GOOD EITHER!

BOO TO

THE BILLYS ARE BONEHEADS

YAH! WE'RE NOT SCARED!

AIM!

WE'LL VENTILATE YOU VARMINTS.

But—

HO-HO!

HA-HA!

BANG! BANG! BANG! BANG!

A laugh or two with you-know-who!

THAT DOES IT! YOU'VE ASKED FOR IT NOW.

I'LL SHOW THAT PEST!

BOWLING GREEN

GRANDAD, COULD YOU DO ME A FAVOUR..?

Soon—

I'LL BET MY GRANDAD COULD BOWL YOU OUT!

I'D LIKE TO SEE HIM TRY!

So—

A BOWLING BALL, EH? I'LL GIVE THIS A GOOD SWIPE.

But— CRACK!

OOF!

HO-HO! WELL DONE, GRANDAD! NOT ONLY DID YOU BOWL HIM OUT—YOU BOWLED HIM OVER AS WELL!

What do you think of Baby Blink?

Baby Crockett

ME'S FED UP BEING BABY CROCKETT.

ME WISHES ME WAS LIKE SOME OF THE OTHER BEEZER CHARACTERS.

ME'S GOOD AS COLONEL BLINK.

CAN'T GET A TUNE OUT OF YOUR BARREL ORGAN, EH? YOUR MONKEY LOOKS WELL ENOUGH.

YOU'RE THE CHEEKY MONKEY.

HA-HA! ME KNOWS! ME COULD BE SCRAPPER.

ALL ME NEEDS IS MUM'S WIG AND A TOUGH LOOK.

OKAY, YOU GUYS. PUT 'EM UP.

WHAT?

OW! ME COULDN'T BE SCRAPPER. ME'S GOT NO HEAD FOR HEIGHTS.

The funniest arrest in the wild and woolly West!

Soon after—

And—

Then—

Then—

And—

When Pop gets curious, the fun's fast and furious!

POP DICK and Harry

THUMP! THUMP! BANG!

WOW! WHAT'S ALL THAT NOISE?

I'LL TAKE A PEEP THROUGH THE KEYHOLE.

LOOK AT THAT SMOKE. I'LL BET IT'S FROM POP'S PIPE. HE'S SPYING ON US.

OOPS! SORRY, POP. I DIDN'T KNOW YOU WERE THERE.

OUCH!

OOH! THAT HURT!

VROOM!

HM! WHAT'S THAT NOISE OUTSIDE?

I'LL JUST PEEK THROUGH THE BLINDS.

HEH! I'LL LOOK THROUGH THESE KNOT-HOLES.

Then—

HELLO, POP. LOOKING FOR US?

ERK!

GRR! YOU IDIOTS! MY NOSE IS STUCK. PULL ME OUT!

OKAY, POP.

And—

OH, DEAR! THAT PLANK'S COME OFF THE SHED WITH YOU, POP.

SHAME!

OH, NO! I CAN'T GET IT OFF!

HA-HA!

HEE-HEE!

Later—

HO-HO! I'LL BET POP WON'T BE SO NOSEY AGAIN!

GRRR!